THE ACA LEGAL SERIES

Volume 7

"LEGAL ISSUES IN MARRIAGE AND FAMILY COUNSELING"

THE ACA LEGAL SERIES:

Series Editor: Theodore P. Remley, Jr., JD, PhD

THE ACA LEGAL SERIES

Volume 7

"LEGAL ISSUES IN MARRIAGE AND FAMILY COUNSELING"

Patricia Stevens-Smith, PhD
Marcia M. Hughes, JD

Series Editor
Theodore P. Remley, Jr., JD, PhD

Copyright © 1993 by the American Counseling Association

American Counseling Association
5999 Stevenson Avenue
Alexandria, VA 22304-3300

Cover design by Sarah Jane Valdez

Library of Congress Cataloging-in-Publication Data

Stevens-Smith, Patricia.
    Legal issues in marriage and family counseling / Patricia Stevens-Smith, Marcia M. Hughes
    p. cm.
    Includes bibliographical references.
    ISBN 1-55620-104-4
    1. Domestic relations—United States. 2. Family counselors—Legal status, laws, etc.—United States. 3. Marriage counselors—Legal status, laws, etc.—United States. 4. Counseling—Law and legislation—United States. I. Hughes, Marcia M. II. Title.
KF505.S85 1993
346.7301'5—dc20
[347.30615]   92-31486
                                                                   CIP
                                    The ACA Legal Series, Volume 7

Printed in the United States of America

To our husbands and families . . . and all families everywhere.

Contents

Biographies

Patricia Stevens-Smith is assistant professor and program director for marriage and family training at the University of Colorado at Denver. She regularly teaches graduate-level marriage and family theory and techniques courses and seminars in professional/ethical issues and works as a private practitioner in Boulder, Colorado. Her research and writing have focused on ethical and legal concerns in counseling and therapy, family health and pathology, and gender issues in counseling. Dr. Stevens-Smith was selected as Outstanding Teacher of the Year within the School of Education at the University of Colorado at Denver. As part of her professional work, she is the national workshop presenter for the American Counseling Association (ACA) on Counseling Today's Families. She is a licensed professional counselor, a Clinical Member of the American Association for Marriage and Family Therapy (AAMFT), and a National Certified Counselor; and she has served on the Licensure Committee for ACA.

Recent publications by Dr. Stevens-Smith include a book entitled *Issues and Topics in Family Therapy* and articles on healthy family functioning, gender issues in training family therapists, the practice of family counseling, and a critique of feminist family therapy.

Marcia M. Hughes has been an attorney in private practice for 16 years and is working on her master's degree in marriage and family therapy. Ms. Hughes received her JD with honors in 1976 from the George Washington University National Law Center. She has been named in Who's Who in American Law for 1992–1993. Ms. Hughes was recently appointed by the president of the Colorado Senate to serve on the Task Force on Family Issues. She is vice-chairperson for public affairs to the Kempe Children's Foundation. Ms. Hughes was selected Big Sister of the year for the greater Denver metropolitan area in 1991. She has been a past chairperson of the Colorado Bar Association's Environmental Law Committee. She also served as chairperson of the Colorado Hazardous Waste Committee, a gubernatorial appointment, and on committees to Governor Lamm's Water Roundtable. Ms. Hughes worked as special assistant to the executive director of the Colorado Department of Health, served as an assistant attorney general in Colorado, and clerked on the 10th Circuit Court of Appeals. She is a stepmother and a foster mother.

Theodore P. Remley, Jr., Series Editor, is Executive Director of the American Counseling Association. Immediately prior to assuming this position, Dr. Remley was chair of the Department of Counselor Education at Mississippi State University in Starkville. He holds a PhD from the Department of Counselor Education at the University of Florida in Gainesville and a JD in law from the Catholic University of America in Washington, DC.

Preface

Many legal issues are pivotal to family concerns brought into therapy. To respond effectively, professional counselors who work with couples and families are experiencing an increasing need to understand some of the basic parameters of family law. As a result of counseling their clients, marriage and family counselors may be asked to produce records, testify regarding counseling sessions, or testify as an expert witness. They may also choose to pursue involvement in evaluating child custody or in divorce mediation.

There are many areas that may bring a family and, therefore, their counselor into the legal system. Families may be involved in legal proceedings as foster parents or adoptive parents. Divorce requires legal proceedings of varying degrees. Custody decisions concerning children may bring parents back to court after the divorce is final. If there is an allegation of child abuse or neglect, another type hearing and evaluation is necessary. Or the children themselves may lead the family into court through juvenile delinquency. These are only some of the recognized areas that bring families and therapists into court.

The importance of marriage and family counselors having a working knowledge of the family laws of their own state cannot be overemphasized. Family law is primarily left to the policy determinations of each state rather than being a matter of federal law. Thus the therapist needs to become familiar with his or her own state's laws. This may be done in part by working with and reviewing the law with a competent local attorney and through reading the newspaper and consultations with peers. Being informed concerning decisions of individual judges in your community is an important aspect because individual judges are generally given a great deal of latitude in making decisions related to families.

This monograph focuses on practical information and offers guidelines for professional counselors who practice marriage and family counseling. It discusses the importance of specialized training for professional counselors to ensure working ethically with couples and families, and it reviews divorce, child custody, and child abuse and neglect, which are some of the most common areas encountered by marriage and family therapists. The various responses a therapist may make if the divorce attorney calls are discussed, and the difference between a family therapist and a divorce mediator is examined. Suggestions for the therapist who testifies as a lay witness or as an expert witness are included. The child abuse and neglect mandatory reporting issue and the rights of stepparents are reviewed. Insurance fraud is discussed. Finally, potential consequences of using paradoxical therapy with the family are presented.

There is great variety in the configuration of today's couples and families, including same sex couples. These couples may face many of the same issues that are addressed in this monograph. However, since the legal system in this country recognizes the heterosexual couple almost exclusively, this monograph uses pronouns reflecting the heterosexual couple.

Many professional counselors today work with couples and families in a variety of settings. In this monograph the terms *professional counselor*, *marriage and family counselor*, and *marriage and family therapist* are used interchangeably. Also used are both *counseling* and *therapy* as terms to refer to the process of facilitating change in clients. The authors wish to emphasize emphatically their commitment to the specialized training necessary to work with couples and families. It is unethical to work beyond one's competence and skill level.

In addition to using their skills in the mental health settings, counselors/therapists are in a position to assist legal and public policy decision makers greatly in understanding new and appropriate ways to respond to families. In order to do so, counselors may participate in legislative or other forums to assist in making decisions responsive to the phenomenal changes facing

families today. The authors believe that as professional counselors who work with families, it is important to be actively
involved in the larger system of society.

Glossary

Alternative Dispute Resolution: A process of reaching a decision that is, or otherwise could be, ultimately addressed by a court. The alternative dispute resolution process can result in a proposed order that a judge, or other authorized official, then signs. Examples of alternative dispute resolution processes include mediation and arbitration.

Arbitration: A voluntary process in which the arbitrator, who is selected to have authority to administer the process and make the decisions, works under the terms of a particular agreement. Arbitration is a more authoritative process than mediation but still more flexible than a court proceeding.

Court Order: A decision issued by a court and signed and dated by a judge or an official entitled to represent the judge, such as a magistrate.

Contested Divorce: In the legal sense, a divorce process handled partially or wholly in the courts under the strict rules of the law without taking advantage of mediation or arbitration to resolve the controversies.

Custody: As used in this monograph, the legal responsibility by an adult for a child. Generally, it is applied in a divorce situation when a determination is made as to which of the spouses will have custody, that is, physical and legal responsibility for the child or children.

Types of custody, which include sole, split, and joint, are in transition in the United States. **Sole custody** is still the most commonly used form of custody upon dissolution of marriage. With sole custody, one parent has the legal and physical responsibility for the child while the noncustodial parent generally has visitation rights and may have child support responsibilities. Significantly, the noncustodial parent may not have a voice in important decisions affecting the child. **Split custody** refers to one parent having custody of one or more children and the remaining children being in the custody of the other parent. Due to the desire to keep children in the same home, split custody is rarely favored by the courts. **Joint custody** generally refers to joint physical and legal custody. However, one parent may be the sole physical custodian with the other having visitation and decision-making rights. The key factor is that both parents retain legal responsibility and authority for the care and decisions related to the child. Key decisions that both parents are generally legally entitled to make include an equal voice in the child's education, religious decisions, and medical care.

Divorce Counseling: A type of therapy in which either one or both divorcing spouses are assisted in working through the psychological problems related to the divorce. It is possible that the divorce therapist may also work with one or both spouses in reaching many of the decisions that are reflected in the final divorce decree ordered by the court. One of the most contentious areas in divorce counseling is child custody.

Divorce Decree: The final order issued, signed, and dated by the judge that sets forth the governing principles of the divorce. Set forth, for example, is what type of custody and visitation is permitted. If one or both members of a couple return to court for modification of the original provisions of their divorce, it is the rules in this decree that one or both are seeking to have changed so that a modified decree can be issued.

Expert Witness: Individuals who have specialized knowledge or experience who could help a judge or jury in coming to a final decision in a lawsuit. Such a witness must first be acknowledged by the presiding judge as one who has specialized knowledge or expertise. Once the expert witness has been acknowledged, he or she may render expert opinions regarding matters in controversy at a hearing or trial.

Fraud: When a person intentionally distorts the truth for the purpose of convincing another to rely upon an untruthful statement in order to gain something valuable or to surrender a legal right. Fraud is discussed in this monograph in the context of misreporting to an insurance company that some type of counseling session occurred that did not actually occur. Committing fraud is a violation of the law and may carry severe legal sanctions.

Lay Witness: A lay witness is any person who is not an expert brought into court specifically to testify as an witness. The lay witness may be testifying voluntarily or be compelled to testify. A lay witness may relate only factual information and may not give opinions.

Malpractice: As applied to a therapist, professional misconduct or unreasonable lack of skill in providing or failing to provide professional services.

Mediation: A form of alternative dispute resolution in which a couple works with a neutral mediator in a process separate from the adversarial system of court-based litigation to seek resolution of some or all issues necessary for the divorce to be completed. The decisions that may be addressed include custody of children, child support payments, and division of property. The mediation may be conducted by a trained mediator who may be a therapist, a lawyer, or someone trained from another profession. Mediation is intended to be a cooperative process, usually entered into on a voluntary basis.

Negligence: Generally the failure of a therapist to use reasonable care and caution or the failure to exercise the degree of care that a prudent person, or a reasonably careful person, should exercise. This may apply to a specific act or a failure to act.

Notice of Deposition: The subpoena.

Psychological Divorce: When a spouse has moved through the separation process from the other spouse to the point of having a greater ability to move forward with his or her life. This may or may not coincide with the legal divorce.

Psychological/Extended Family of Children: Significant others, be they adults or children, to whom children may be psychologically or emotionally attached, even though there is no legal familial relationship as established by blood or marriage. Courts are beginning to give further recognition and credence to the importance to children of their psychological families.

Subpoena: A court document that orders a person to appear in court for a hearing or trial or at another location to be questioned regarding a pending lawsuit. Persons receiving a subpoena must comply unless the subpoena is withdrawn or is overruled by a judge. The penalty for noncompliance may include incarceration in jail or a fine.

Third Parties: Someone indirectly related to the issue before the court who may not have independent authority to ask a court to take a particular action. Stepparents are often considered third parties in a custody action. The "parties" are the natural parents.

Training, Practice, and Licensure

In view of the growing number of individuals practicing marriage and family counseling, the issue of appropriate training is increasingly important. Marriage and family counseling/therapy requires specialized skills that may not be taught in other mental health areas. To place an individual without these skills into a family session might well be construed as practicing beyond the person's area of competence (Margolin, 1982) and has legal implications for the professional counselor.

Professional training of marriage and family counselors/therapists may take place in several ways. A first and most formal method is through a master's or doctoral-level program in an accredited college or university. Psychology, counseling, and social work programs may have marriage and family training components within their program areas. A second method of training is an extension of the counselor's degree in the mental health field either through independent university studies or workshops.

No matter how therapists receive their training, it is imperative that they meet the legal requirements to practice marriage and family counseling within their state. In 1991, 38 states licensed the practice of professional counseling, and 26 states regulated the practice of marriage and family therapy. In general these states require a minimum of a master's degree in counseling, marriage and family therapy, social work, pastoral counseling, or relevant qualifications in related fields. States differ in their requirements for supervised experience. Passing a written examination is also required. Some states require that individuals participate in continuing education in order to renew their license or certification. Because state laws and regulation vary, it is important to be aware of your own state's laws and regulatory requirements in this area. For example, in California, which requires that an individual hold the appropriate licensure, a licensed psychologist who calls him- or herself a marriage and family counselor also has to be licensed as a child, marriage, and family counselor. Some states exempt individuals practicing within the guidelines of another professional licensure as long as they do not claim to practice or to be licensed as a marriage and family therapist (Huber & Baruth, 1987).

If you are a licensed professional counselor, psychiatrist, psychologist, or social worker, you may see couples and families within the framework of your agency or practice. You must represent yourself and your training in an accurate manner to your client in order to avoid legal complications. The appropriate place for this information to be presented to your client is in your disclosure form and in your first session with the client. Some states require that a disclosure statement with this information be given to the client. Additionally, some states require that the disclosure statement be on file with the appropriate state licensing board.

Another area of legal concern is diagnosis. The majority of third-party payment sources base their payment criteria upon the *Diagnostic and Statistical Manual of Mental Disorders* (DSMIII-R) (American Psychiatric Association, 1987). This medical model of assessment and diagnosis is individually oriented. For marriage and family counselors this may present an ethical as well as a legal dilemma. In addition to focusing the pathology on an individual family member, this type of assessment and diagnosis is contrary to the philosophy of marriage and family theory, which focuses on holistic wellness.

Insurance companies, however, will not reimburse for services rendered unless the DSMIII-R is used to categorize the individual. It behooves the marriage and family counselor to be clear as to the type of therapy, who is being treated, and the implications of diagnosis for the client. The counselor may well explain to the client why diagnosis is necessary and the implications of the diagnosis.

If the marriage and family counselor is seeing the whole family but billing the insurance company for an individual diagnosis, this may be considered fraud by the insurance company. Mental health professionals place themselves at risk of legal prosecution as well as of ethical censure by their professional organization by this procedure.

Supervision is highly recommended in both training and continued practice of marriage and family counseling. Supervision through means of a one-way mirror or audio- and videotaping of sessions is encouraged (Berger & Dammon, 1982). The legal implications of this type of supervision are apparent. Permission from all individuals participating in the session MUST be in writing prior to the beginning of the session.

Working with substance abusers is another area in which marriage and family counselors/therapists need to be knowledgeable of the restrictions concerning confidentiality, the ethical right of clients from unauthorized release of information, and privileged communication, the legal right that protects a client from having information revealed publicly (see Arthur & Swanson, 1992). Federal law strictly regulates the method and amount of information that can be given concerning someone who is in treatment for substance abuse. If the therapist is working with a family that has a substance abusing member, the federal guidelines concerning confidentiality must be observed.

Presently it appears that the specialty of marriage and family counseling is governed more by professional organizations than by statute, but this is in transition. The legal governance of marriage and family therapy is being strengthened. Additionally, the legal restraints that apply to all helping professions apply to marriage and family counseling/therapy. These are:

- duty to warn
- duty to report child abuse and neglect (and perhaps elder abuse)
- maintenance of confidentiality
- use of accepted methods of counseling
- honest representation of your qualifications and training to your clients
- informed consent and disclosure.

All mental health professionals today need to be familiar with both federal and state laws that affect families, as well as with mental health law. Issues such as divorce, child custody, abuse and neglect, and family violence fall under the auspices of family law. In order to avoid legal difficulties and to best serve the client, therapists should be current on these areas of law. Remember, however, that it is considered unethical and illegal to give legal advice to your client in any of these areas, that the counselor/therapist is opening the door for civil action and censure if he or she gives legal advice.

In summary, professional counselors must be competently trained in the type of counseling that they practice. Licensure provides minimum standards of practice and also assures some protection for both the client and the therapist in legal matters.

What to Do When a Divorce Attorney Calls You

Marriage and family counselors frequently work with couples who are considering, currently are involved in, or may later enter into divorce proceedings. What should the therapist do when the divorce attorney calls? First, do *not* respond to any questions without written permission from the client(s) or without a court order to respond. Many therapists will not even acknowledge knowing the client(s) without receiving permission from the client(s) first. If in doubt, call your attorney for advice. A small amount of help initially can prevent a lot of trouble later.

Under most state laws, clients are entitled to their records, which is consistent with the current trend to empower consumers. Thus if a client asks you to provide information to his or her divorce attorney and your client is an individual, providing the records is not only legally appropriate but also ethical. However, for a professional counselor who has worked with both the husband and wife, the case may not be as clear. Consent is ethically necessary from all parties involved in a session before the information can be released, unless there is a court order. If you counseled both spouses but only one authorizes release of the information, it is important for you to know your state law to determine how to respond. Is each one individually entitled to all the records from each session, only the records explicitly having to do with him or her if they are severable, or none of the records unless all adults have agreed? Should the state law be uncertain on this matter, we suggest your disclosure statement clearly state that release by all parties is required. Your disclosure statement should recognize that you are working with both a husband and wife together as the client, that records will be released only with dual consent or by court order, and that you will testify only if *both* parties request such action or if ordered to do so by the court. This procedure gives you the maximum protection and best recognizes your respect for both clients.

If you do not have a signed consent from both clients to provide information to a particular attorney, it is best not to do so. You may tell the attorney that you do not have permission to talk at this time. One might state to the attorney "If this person were my client, I would not be authorized to discuss information with you unless I had been given a signed release to do so." The exception to this is if the information is required by court order, which is a document signed by the judge ordering a particular action or event.

If the attorney attempts in any way to persuade you to give the information without the person's written permission, it is best simply to adhere to the standards just stated. Should the provisions allowing you to release information not be in place, the divorce attorney has an alternative pursuant to the law. She or he may go back to the client or clients, get written permission, and then provide it to you. It may be helpful to promote mutual understanding with the attorney by saying, "I know you experience the same ethical constraints against releasing information without written permission from your clients." This contact may be the last you have with the divorce lawyer if adequate permission for you to communicate further is not given.

Under most state laws you are required to release information if the clients provide informed consent. Such informed consent is most clearly available if both clients (1) have signed a request that you talk with named attorney or attorneys and provide information and (2) have specifically discussed the content of the information to be given to the attorney. If these two elements are not present, it may be more prudent for you not to answer the questions of the divorce attorney.

If the attorney wants information you have not been given permission to provide, you may receive a subpoena. The elements of subpoena and how to respond to a subpoena are set forth in the monograph *Preparing for Court Appearances* (Remley, 1991). In essence, if you receive a subpoena that also requires you to bring records you have three obligations: (1) to appear with the documents, (2) to notify your clients, and (3) to wait for a court order unless you have the client's permission to release the documents. Your client may have an interest in opposing release of the information. Thus it is most important for him or her to know as soon as possible about the subpoena. It is important for you as the counselor to remember that you are not a "party"; that is, the counselor is not a proponent for the decision that someone is seeking from a judge, nor is the counselor an opponent. The counselor is simply someone with information that might be relevant. Your role is as a provider of information, not as an advocate.

If you testify at a hearing, the attorney for the other side probably will cross-examine you. Above all, do not take the cross-examiner's manner of questioning or type of question personally. The cross-examination reflects what the attorney thinks he or she needs to do to prove the case. Remember that the legal system is designed as an adversarial system and that the opposing attorney is only doing the job required of him or her.

Although the subpoena may set a specific time when you are to provide the information, the attorney may be willing to reschedule if you cannot be available. However, if you do not have your clients' consent, you may decide not to provide documents without a court order. You must show up at the time and place the subpoena establishes; but you are not legally required at that time to turn over documents unless a judge orders you to do so.

If you are subpoenaed, remember these four practical guidelines:

1. Subpoenas may specifically set forth the date, time, and place to appear or present records, but there often is flexibility. Thus you may call the attorney to schedule a better time.
2. If only records have been subpoenaed and testimony is not subpoenaed, many states allow you to file a sealed copy of the records with the court to be produced at the appropriate mo-

ment. Of course, you do this only if you have verified the client's informed consent to disclosure of the records. Otherwise, you have to wait for a court order. If consent is in place and you can simply file the sealed copy, you may save yourself a great deal of time and effort.

3. Copies of the subpoenaed records and notes should be made. You should retain originals if at all possible.

4. *Never* alter or destroy a document that has been subpoenaed. The potential adverse consequences of such an action can not be underestimated. This is the one way that the therapist can become personally involved, and it will be only to your detriment (Group for the Advancement of Psychiatry, 1991).

If you have been subpoenaed to testify, you will be testifying as a lay witness (Remley, 1991). This type of witness is also referred to as a factual or a general witness. Your only responsibility is to report your professional impression of what occurred in the past.

The Marriage and Family Counselor as an Expert Witness

Courts are increasingly recognizing the influence a family plays in a wide variety of matters that come to the court's attention. Thus the role for the marriage and family counselor as an expert witness is expanding. Some of the ways in which a marriage and family counselor may be an expert witness are in addressing juvenile treatment, child custody disputes, dependency and neglect matters, and competency matters or in determining whether a child should be removed from the home temporarily or permanently in situations where there has been an allegation of child abuse. Professional counselors are more likely to testify in civil proceedings, but their expertise could also be required in criminal matters.

When a marriage and family counselor is called upon to testify as an expert witness, he or she is appointed by the court explicitly for the purpose of preparing and providing an opinion in court in a thorough and professional manner. When professional counselors serve as expert witnesses, they should be impartial and not act as an advocate for either position. The expert is defined as someone who is specifically hired to "formulate a presented opinion in court based on [his or her] specialized knowledge of mental health" (Remley, 1991, p. 39).

Testifying as an expert witness is a particular type of task with specific differences from a counseling session. Thus, it is important that the therapist understand what is required of an expert witness before a decision is made to assume this role. It requires working with the legal system, which includes attorneys and judges. Because there are different orientations between the counseling system and the legal system, the therapist must decide that working to create cooperation between these two systems is appropriate to be successful in this role. The counselor must use his or her highest level of professionalism throughout employment as an expert. Testimony may directly influence the result of a legal proceeding. Furthermore, the quality of your presentation will influence your individual reputation as well as the general reputation of marriage and family counselors. No matter how large a city or small a village you work in, your work as a professional will be remembered by those participating in the arena in which you work.

Meyerstein and Todd (1980) emphasized the ways in which marriage and family therapists can use their particular awareness of family systems to be even more effective in the court room. They particularly suggested using the strategic understandings of redefining or reframing the problem and dealing with resistance. The therapist as an expert witness can present his or her testimony in a persuasive teaching or advocacy way by using reframing (Huber & Baruth, 1987). Similarly, a court room can certainly seem like a place of resistance, particularly when the therapist is under cross-examination. Responding to resistance as you might work with a client can be an effective therapy with the "resisting" cross-examining attorney.

The specific steps that an expert may take from the first interview to the conclusion of the case should be evaluated in materials relevant to that particular area of law. Consulting with peers who have already been employed as expert witnesses is also a good way of gaining an understanding of the process.

The first step toward being an expert witness may be an attorney contacting the counselor and asking if he or she is interested in being an expert witness in a particular matter. Counselors also may initiate the contact by asking attorneys who use expert witnesses if they ever have a need for marriage and family counselors. Once this contact occurs, the counselor should:

- Seek background information on the attorney as well as the client. If you do not know the attorney, you might check with peers to get better information.
- Check for confidentiality concerns. Have you been involved with these clients before? If so, take all steps necessary to make sure that you are authorized to be involved in this proceeding and clarify what information you are allowed to use. Some take the position, though it is not required, that a counselor should not take an expert witness case if he or she has had any previous contact with the matter. Others disagree. If the therapist has represented the clients before, he or she should obtain their written permission to be involved in the matter as well as to disclose information and your records from the past.
- Clarify how the attorney intends to move through the proceeding. Find out, for example, when the pretrial date is, when the trial is scheduled, and whether depositions are anticipated. Be sure you can meet the time schedule. Determine how much the attorney will work directly with you. Particularly if it is a complex case, you may need to meet with the attorney several times.
- Clarify with the attorney how he or she will work with you on your written report, if one is required. Draft your written document first, discuss it with the attorney, and then finalize it. It is important for everyone to understand you will not change your opinion in order to meet the attorney's or client's particular needs. Review by the attorney of the content and format of your report in order to put it in the context of the case can be most valuable.
- Have a written contract under which you are hired that spells out all details that are important to you. Be certain you describe how and when you are to be paid.

Your work will require several specific steps with details relevant to the type of proceeding in which you are involved, including reviewing the case and understanding the background facts; having a general familiarity with the law relevant to this particular type of matter so that you understand the context in which you are asked to testify; having a general understanding of the rules of evidence that will apply in court; and understanding the general dialectic nature of the court system and how you are expected to respond under direct testimony, cross-examination, and re-direct examination.

Be sure your attorney works with you if you are not a seasoned expert. Even if you are a seasoned expert, remember that each court has its own nuances. The attorney should be available to work with you to prepare your testimony and to understand your presentation in this particular court room.

After reviewing the case and acquiring a general understanding of this area of law and how the matter will proceed in this particular court, you will be meeting with the client to conduct your examination. The attorney should understand that several sessions may be necessary and that psychological or other tests may be required. Work with the attorney regarding where the examination will occur.

After meeting with the client, prepare your report and meet with the attorney about the report. A specific, detailed report format may be expected in this particular area of law. Be certain that you use the expected format and that your report is of the highest professional quality in its content. Ask the attorney for a copy of similar testimony or confer with peers if you are not already familiar with the expectations. Finally, move forward into preparing for your actual testimony in court. Meet with the attorney so that you will understand the process of direct testimony, cross-examination, and re-direct.

Being an expert witness can be highly rewarding. However, the role of the counselor is quite different in the courtroom than in the counseling session. It is important to be thoroughly prepared for this new role.

Divorce Mediation and Counseling

Couples enter counseling for many purposes. Frequently it is to seek help because a decision to divorce has already been made or is being considered. Seeking counseling can greatly assist couples in moving through this traumatic time and in finding an acceptable resolution to their conflict. Professional assistance for the divorcing couple is available in different forms. Two types of assistance are therapy and mediation, and there can be substantial overlap between the therapist's role as a divorce therapist and the role as a divorce mediator.

There are ethical constraints around the practice of counseling and even more around the practice of law that can limit the flexibility of what may occur in either therapy or mediation. However, many divorce decisions, such as property settlement, custody arrangement, and even the more emotional aspects of divorce, can be mediated by a therapist or an attorney. Key questions then become, What is the client's goal in coming to see you? What type of assistance are you qualified to provide?

The divorce process can be viewed as a continuum moving from the least to the most controversial or contentious. This can be measured by the degree to which the divorce decisions can be settled by the parties rather than by someone else such as the judge. The least controversial is an *uncontested divorce*, in which the parties reach the decisions themselves and the settlement document is simply filed with the court for a judge's signature. There is generally a given waiting period before the judge signs the document. A divorce cannot occur without some legal action; therefore, a judge's approval is required, though there may not be a hearing.

The second level is a *mediated divorce*, in which the couple receives assistance but still jointly works to reach the answers through some form of compromise that the court approves. The third level is an *arbitrated divorce*, which exhibits increasing rules and less self-determination by the parties of the divorce decision. Arbitration is a voluntary process in which an authority figure—the arbitrator (usually an attorney)—works under the terms of a particular agreement and may make specific decisions based upon that agreement (Spencer & Zammit, 1976). According to the agreement reached through arbitration, the final result may have many different effects. The decision could be binding, carrying the same weight as a court decision; it could be part of a settlement agreement; or it could be an advisory document the court could assess (Herrmann, McKenry, & Weber, 1979). Although arbitration is an authoritative process, it is usually much more flexible than a court proceeding.

Finally, there is the fully *contested divorce*, which at its most extreme does not include any form of mediated or arbitrated resolution of the controversies. *Contested* implies a high degree of disagreement. The parties are not able to settle the decisions themselves. In a contested divorce the decision is turned over to the legal system. This process usually reflects dependency and low commitment to the decision (Herrmann et al., 1979). If a divorce is fully litigated, it is likely that neither party is committed to implementing the divorce decree. Areas such as child custody provisions may not be successfully implemented. The likelihood of returning to court for further challenges, especially concerning custody, is high (Pearson & Thoennes, 1982).

The best results for individuals occur when the couple is able to achieve a psychological divorce and a legal divorce simultaneously. However, even if couples can psychologically divorce, divorce remains a legal action, and the law must therefore be involved to some degree.

As already noted, the divorce process can be viewed as a continuum:

Type of Divorce:	Uncontested	Mediated	Arbitrated	Contested

Role of therapist:

Role of attorney:

The therapist has a more direct role when there is less legal conflict, as with the uncontested divorce. The counselor's role lessens in the divorce proceeding as the action becomes more contested. It is the inverse for a lawyer, who is likely to be much less involved, if at all, in an uncontested proceeding and heavily involved in the contested proceeding. It is important for clients who have decided on divorce to examine the following areas in relation to how involved personally and/or legally they want to become. That is, each party needs to determine the level of personal/legal involvement that will:

- best allow him or her to divorce psychologically
- be best for the children
- settle the issues acceptably
- not lead to efforts to amend the custody or other decisions.

Fisher and Fisher (1982) advised lawyers and therapists to work together with divorcing spouses. Both professions seek to help their clients, but in different ways. In counseling, the therapist helps the client learn how to help her- or himself. The lawyer works with the client so that the client chooses between alternatives, and it is the lawyer who then acts rather than the client.

Certainly the counselor, mediator, and the lawyer have overlapping roles in this process. It is important to gain as much understanding of each role as possible so the benefits of all professions can be made available to the client. A client may authorize the therapist and lawyer to cooperate for the client's benefits. This is the ideal situation.

Law and counseling come closest in the area of mediation. *Mediation* is generally defined as a form of alternative dispute resolution in which a couple works with a neutral mediator in a process separate from the adversarial system of litigation to seek resolution of the divorce dispute. Gold (1981) noted that mediation "can be seen as an attempt to redefine the adversary nature of legal proceedings, provide a means by which the needs and well-being of all family members can be supported, and lay the foundation for the cooperative evolution of new family structures" (p. 9). The key to mediation is that parties reach a voluntary compromise to which they are more committed than to a court-imposed decision (Spencer & Zammit, 1976). Mediation is an arena of opportunity for counselors to assist clients in making congruent decisions to support the clients' lives and implement their values.

The benefits possible from mediation are numerous. According to Weaver (1986), the benefits available from mediation when compared to litigation include:

- reaching resolution earlier, through, for example, pretrial agreements
- higher satisfaction with the divorce agreements
- reduced returns to court to renegotiate settlement or custody
- increased joint custody agreements
- overall therapeutic value for the divorcing couple.

The method by which the agreement is reached is important. The mediation process can generate a sense of equality and can promote better understanding and communication between the former spouses. Some evaluators have found that the more the mediator can assist the couple in being empathic with one another, the better the result. Another important benefit of mediation is that someone is working for the "often powerless" third party, the child (Hopkins, 1982; Pearson & Thoennes, 1982; Slaikeu, Culler, Pearson, & Thoennes, 1985).

The mediation process includes the following stages:

1. **Setting the stage**. The purpose of this stage is to provide a neutral setting, establish ground rules, and get the participants' commitment.
2. **Defining the issues**. Clients discuss their needs and feelings.
3. **Processing the issues**. In this stage clients learn to manage emotions, show empathy, and explore solutions.
4. **Reaching a settlement** (Huber & Baruth, 1987).

The goals and strategies a divorce counselor or a mediator use in working with a divorcing couple overlap and can be joined successfully by the mediator.

According to Weaver (1986), an important similarity between divorce therapy and mediation is that the therapist and mediator both need to establish an effective relationship that includes the components of building trust, maintaining impartiality, and diagnosing the marital conflict. Other components necessary for process facilitation in mediation are maintaining control of the sessions by being directive; attempting to equalize balance between the parties; incorporating a constant sense of reality when the couples discuss their concerns; and assisting in the actual separation agreement. The mediator may also provide support and empathy, aiding the clients in clarifying their needs and values, expressing feelings, and exploring ambivalence. Advancing self-determination and autonomy, and continuing the parental role are also important goals of mediation.

A divorce process recommended by Spencer and Zammit (1976) is a three-stage model that begins with therapy, moves to mediation and then ends with arbitration, if necessary. The first stage involves working with a family counseling specialist who assists in drafting a separation agreement. That same specialist participates in a required mediation process when disputes arise under the agreement. The second stage is mediation and occurs only if necessary. If mediation cannot resolve matters, then the third stage involves submission to arbitration. The process ends at whatever level full agreement is reached.

Generally, there are no specific requirements governing the training of a mediator. Thus the mediator may be a trained therapist, a trained lawyer, someone trained in other areas such as communications, or a combination of these. The goal of mediation is to assist the couple in simultaneously achieving a psychological and a legal divorce. The mediator can best serve the clients by understanding the basics of both therapy and the law. It is essential, though, for mediators—as well as counselors—to understand the limits of assistance to be provided, to understand where their expertise stops and that it never includes giving legal advice. The unlicensed practice of law is illegal. Many questions relating to legal rights are likely to be raised during mediation. Those questions must ethically and legally be referred to an attorney. It is a common and ethical practice for the mediator to recommend that the husband and wife each have their own divorce attorney.

In addition to dealing with the specific decisions regarding custody rights and responsibilities and property division, most of the issues in the mediation sessions are likely to relate to the family system, that is, to family functioning and communication, and how this stressful process of divorce can be handled most effectively. Judge Woolley (1986), in describing an experimental court-based mediation process in California, made an important statement: "Judges dissolve marriages—not families" (p. 2). Families continue after a divorce, only in a different configuration.

If there is a divorce, there is a decree or order signed by the judge. If the decree is based on the mediated agreement between the couple, it appears that the mediation was effective.

What the therapist's level of involvement should be in developing a separation agreement is an important question. Much of the agreement, as well as the psychological impact of separation, can be addressed in therapy or mediation. It is essential, however, that both the husband and wife understand the legal consequences of their decisions through discussion with someone trained in the law.

The most significant caveat for the divorce counselor is that the therapist must have a good understanding of the state's legal system in order to best assist the clients. Furthermore, it is essential that the therapist know when to turn questions over to a lawyer and never to give legal advice. The filing and final drafting of the separation agreement and the divorce settlement are particularly appropriate areas for the attorneys.

Child Custody Evaluation

Determinations regarding child custody both at the time of divorce and when brought back for potential amendment are often difficult cases for judges. The judge must determine what is best for the child or the children. The testimony presented by the two parents is obviously weighted toward what each parent wants. Yet the standard employed is that the court makes a determination in "the best interests of the child." To make this determination, judges often rely on the testimony of expert witnesses, including professional counselors. Thus it is common practice today for a judge to issue an order appointing a child custody evaluator. In such case, the evaluator is perceived to be neutral or objective. The child custody evaluator represents the children and the courts, not the parents. This point is imperative for the parents and the evaluator to understand.

This process gives children a voice in court through the independent advice of the evaluator. Given the reliance the court, the children, and the family place on the competence of the report prepared and presented by the child custody evaluator, it is necessary that the evaluator be professionally prepared to conduct the work and do so within the highest professional standards.

Derdeyn (1989) has concluded that courts can enhance the stability of postdivorce families when unbiased child custody evaluators are used. This is one of the many values resulting from an evaluator's work.

There are several types of custody. These include:

- sole custody, in which only one parent has custody though the other may have visitation rights
- split custody, in which each parent has some of the children
- joint custody, in which both parents retain legal responsibility as well as authority for the care and control of their children.

The specialized knowledge required to be a child custody evaluator includes expertise in child growth and development, family systems, effective parenting, psychometry, counseling, and witness testimony (Remley & Miranti, 1992). Thus the therapist interested in being involved in this area should be sure of training in these areas. Everett and Volgy (1983) presented a team model of family assessment using a male and female therapist team. One of the therapists is designated as the parent/family therapist, and one is designated the child/sibling therapist. The authors contended that the team approach increases objectivity of evaluation. Another approach in child custody cases is to work as a child custody mediator. These sessions are usually scheduled for 2 to 4 hours, 10 to 14 days before the scheduled trial date. They are attended by the parents, their attorneys, a court mediator, and the judge. In this model, the therapist serves as a mediator using the same skills that were outlined in the Divorce Mediation and Counseling chapter.

The child custody evaluator must be aware of the deadlines the court has established so that all work is done on a timely basis. In conducting the evaluation, the ages of the children are particularly important for the design of the process. The evaluation often includes a home visit and specific testing. Maintaining impartiality throughout the process is of the utmost importance.

Children can often be victims in custody litigation. The sensitivity of the child custody evaluator can help change that potential result. Thus it is important to listen to the children, within the context of their age and stage of development, but at the same time to be sure that they do not feel burdened with making the choice between parents (Remley & Miranti, 1992).

The evaluation report often needs to be prepared in a specified manner. When the court appoints you, determine if there is a specific format preferred by that court. This can be done by either asking the judge or peers who have performed similar roles. Furthermore, the judge needs a specific recommendation. Presenting an ambiguous thought process is unhelpful and detrimental. Your recommendations should be substantiated with specific findings supported by evidence.

Remley and Miranti (1992) recommended telling parents your conclusions as a matter of courtesy before submitting the report to the court. Parents must be aware, however, that this is not an opportunity to change your independent conclusions. Additionally, should there be interactions with attorneys during the evaluation process, it is appropriate to answer factual questions. However, do not discuss the report until it is final. If you receive notice of a deposition before you have finalized your report, you may ask the judge to delay your testimony. However, you must follow the order of the judge regardless of the timing.

The art of responding to cross-examination is as important in this type of proceeding as in any other. The attorney of the parent who feels the report is least favorable is likely to challenge the procedure followed in completing your report as well as the conclusions. Prepare for cross-examination through observing other court proceedings, reading relevant articles, and discussing the process with experienced peers and attorneys not involved in this matter. The manner in which you respond in testimony may make a significant difference in how the report is received. Being able to assist the children and the judge as well as assist the development of a final decision with long-term acceptability to the family constitute the rewards for the child custody evaluator.

Child Abuse and Neglect

The U.S. Advisory Board on Child Abuse and Neglect (1990) has declared that the rampant problems in our nation's response to treatment and prevention of child abuse and neglect are so extreme that the issue is a national emergency. This board was established by Congress to evaluate our nation's effectiveness in accomplishing the purposes of the Child Abuse Prevention and Treatment Act of 1974. Most counselors working with families, as well as most other people in our nation, are aware that the incidence of reported child abuse and neglect is growing rapidly.

The significant concern raised by child abuse and neglect is likely to be a matter that many counselors confront. Counselors may be affected not only in the context of the overall health of the society in which they live but also in terms of mandatory requirements to make a report when a counselor suspects child abuse or neglect. Counselors may be involved in working with a family from which a child or children may be temporarily or permanently removed from a home through a dependency and neglect proceeding. Counselors may also testify in criminal actions in which a parent or other caregiver is charged with abuse or neglect.

Many marriage and family counselors also counsel survivors of incest or other affected family members. Davis (1991) estimated that one in four girls and one in seven boys are sexually abused by the time they reach age 18. Given these numbers, the likelihood of a client being directly touched by child abuse and neglect is extremely high. The counselor may be counseling a child who is an incest survivor or who is affected because his or her parent is a survivor, or may be counseling a survivor who is just in the process of remembering his or her childhood abuse.

Counselors must be certain that they have adequate training to address the issues raised by the client. Because these are matters that may go to court, it is critical that the marriage and family counselor pay attention to his or her therapeutic work so that it does not contaminate future legal proceedings. The manner in which a counselor interviews and works with a client could eliminate the ability to conduct successful prosecution. It is critical to prevent this consequence.

There are three general rules to follow when interviewing a potentially abused child: First, record the interview, using videotape if at all possible. This can assist the attorneys in rebutting challenges that the counselor spoon-fed particular answers to the client. Second, avoid using leading questions. Third, if some prompting is necessary in working with the client, do it in the most neutral way possible. In working with a child, the therapist should not say, for example, "Is daddy the one who hurt you?" This suggests the answer to the child and may contaminate the ability to use this as evidence. Furthermore, it is quite possible that daddy is not the one, but a susceptible child may sense that this is an acceptable answer and use it rather than identifying the perpetrator. This has the additional consequence of leaving a child abuser unrestricted and available to hurt other children.

Although our general societal belief is that parents are in the best position to care for a child, the U.S. Supreme Court in *Prince v. Massachusetts* (1944) made it clear that a parent's rights are not absolute. Many state laws provide that a parent-child relationship includes both rights and responsibilities. For example, Colorado provides that the "parent and child relationship means the legal relationship existing between a child and his natural or adoptive parents incident to which the laws confers or imposes rights, privileges, duties, and obligations" (Colorado Revised Statutes 19-4-102).

One specific nationwide action taken to protect children was the adoption of the federal Child Abuse Prevention and Treatment Act of 1974 under which states must require reporting of all forms of child maltreatment in order to receive federal grants (Besharov, 1990). The Act makes reportable "any parental act or omission that harms a child—or threatens to do so" (p. 29). The result of this federal requirement is that nearly every state requires the reporting of all forms of maltreatment whether it is physical, sexual, or emotional. This mandatory reporting is usually required to be done "immediately," though some states set a specific time limit. If your state does not specifically define a time limit or the meaning of *immediate*, we strongly suggest caution in allowing any time to pass before reporting. Also, if a counselor observes a situation that seems to be an emergency, the counselor could be liable if he or she does not report the situation immediately, even if the state law provides additional time.

State laws frequently provide that the reporting may be made either to the county department of social services or to the police department. Furthermore, most laws provide penalties, many of them criminal, for failing to report. Any mandatory reporter, including the counselor, is also vulnerable to being sued for failure to report. Additionally, the negligent failure to report could be found to be professional malpractice. However, all states provide immunity from civil and criminal liability to persons who do report (Besharov, 1990).

Some counselors may balk at this legal requirement, but they should have no doubt that it is a legal requirement that should be taken quite seriously and file a report promptly when necessary. It is important to bear in mind that the mandatory reporting duty usually is imposed when there is reason to know or suspect that a child has been subjected to abuse or neglect or when the child is subjected to circumstances or conditions that could reasonably result in abuse or neglect.

Some counselors are hesitant to comply with the reporting requirements because such action may interfere with their therapeutic relationship with the client. However, the Congress as well as legislatures across the United States have made the decision that child abuse and neglect is not to be kept a secret and that children do deserve to be protected. Thus compliance with the law is nondiscretionary. We recommend that counselors point out the requirement to report in their disclosure statement so that the client will be aware of this limitation on confidentiality. It may also be beneficial to explain to the client how the reporting process works.

There may be many reasons why mandated reporters fail to report incidents of child abuse and neglect. Reasons could include countertransference related to fear, shame, and sympathy (Pollack & Levy, 1989). No matter what the reasons for concern regarding mandatory reporting, however, it is imperative that the counselor address those concerns effectively so that he or she is able to respond to the requirement to protect children by reporting when there is reason to suspect abuse.

Parents may also be involved with local courts in what are generally referred to as dependency and neglect proceedings. Such proceedings could be initiated if reporting has occurred or if the department of social services in any other way finds out that children are—or may be—being abused or neglected. Such proceedings may cause a child to be temporarily or permanently removed from a home through termination of parental rights. A key aspect for the professional counselor during such proceedings is working out a treatment plan in order to assist the entire family. The same federal law that requires mandatory reporting also requires that social service workers use reasonable efforts to assist a family in staying together so that adoption and extensive foster care are not required if possible. The counselor may be involved with the parents in moving through such a proceeding through personal counseling. Other counselors may be involved through their role in working with the department of social services.

Overall, we recommend that counselors stay aware of this area in their community and stay well trained to respond to client needs as they appear. Treatment techniques, the law, and societal awareness are continually evolving in this area of counseling.

Rights and Responsibilities for Stepparents

In today's evolving world of family formations, stepfamilies are a frequent client of professional counselors specializing in marriage and family counseling. Some stepfamily issues may be affected by their relationship with the law. Stepparents may be concerned or frustrated with their legal rights and responsibilities or, more bluntly, their lack of rights. As Pasley (1988) pointed out, the "structural complexity influences the nature of stepfamily interaction" (p. 453). This same structural complexity transfers into the legal picture.

Stepparents are considered third parties in relationship to legal actions affecting their stepchildren. They are not the natural parents and thus have no inherent rights or responsibilities regarding custody, visitation, child support, or many of the other matters that relate in a family situation. However, although stepparents do not have inherent rights, such rights and responsibilities may be granted by legislatures. In some states stepparents' rights and responsibilities are expanding, but there are still many states with no legislation providing any rights or responsibilities.

According to Victor, Robbins, and Bassett (1991), our legal "culture" varies greatly across the states, but family law is becoming more national. These authors suggested that over the next several decades we will come closer to a national consensus in the area they call family issues. Until that happens, step-families will be treated differently in different states.

As with every other area of family law, it is important for marriage and family practitioners to become familiar with their particular state laws relating to stepfamilies. If there is no legis-lation in the state, there is a good possibility that no rights or responsibilities exist. Legal matters that a stepfamily might bring into counseling include interactions related to earlier matters discussed in this monograph, such as how the earlier divorce decree was written regarding custody, visitation, and support. These items may raise tensions and desire for change with the formation of a new family unit. The emotional response to seek-ing these changes is likely to be an issue brought into therapy. Furthermore, participation as a lay witness or as a witness at future custody hearings is a possible role for the marriage and family therapist dealing with stepfamilies.

There are some similarities between the roles for stepparents and grandparents. Grandparents are also third parties, often desiring visitation rights to their grandchildren. By now, all 50 states have some statutory provisions allowing visitation for grandparents. However, the number of states providing for visitation or other rights for stepparents is still much more limited. States developing specific rights are often also looking at the rights of half-brothers and half-sisters. Ten states, char-acterized by Victor, Robbins, and Bassett (1991) as reflecting the "more progressive trend," recognize the "psychological/extended family of children," thus allowing grandparents and others to seek a continued relationship with the child. Hawaii, which has the broadest statute, "provides reasonable visitation rights to parents, grandparents, and any other person interested in the welfare of the child in the discretion of the court, unless it is shown that rights of visitation are detrimental to the best inter-ests of the child" (p. 23). Just as with child custody decisions relating to the breakup of the nuclear family, the same standard of determining the best interests of the child is used in making decisions about the rights or responsibilities of stepparents.

The courts have been most reluctant to impose a legal obliga-tion upon stepparents to support their stepchildren (Knaub, 1986). The attitude of the courts has been that the responsibility to support a child is that of the natural parents, and a stepparent's involvement is purely voluntary. This has been modified in a few states, but only in very limited circumstances. The primary exception is when the stepparent has expressed an intent and acted upon a willingness to assume a parental relationship to the child. Even then, the obligation often terminates at divorce. However, there have been some limited determinations of a legal principle in which the stepparent has been stopped from asserting that he or she no longer has responsibility to the child after divorce or separation (*Miller v. Miller*, 1984). Among those limited circumstances are when the stepparent has supported the child for a significant period of time, acted like a parent to the child, and actively discouraged the relationship with the other natural parent. In such a case, the dependency of the child on the stepparent may be so well developed that the stepparent may not be able to escape support responsibility.

In *Miller v. Miller*, the court stated a stringent test for imposing a permanent support obligation on a stepparent. It is a limited test applying to limited circumstances, so the obligation is seldom imposed. The custodial parent seeking the financial support has the burden of showing that the stepparent made a representation of support to either the custodial parent or the child; that reliance existed; and that statements or conduct of the stepparent led to termination of support by the natural parent.

Many of the clients of marriage and family counselors who are considering second marriages are concerned about matters such as the financial implications of child support payments. Questions such as this should be referred to an attorney for legal advice. If you are aware of competent family lawyers in the area, it is appropriate to give several references.

Another issue relating to stepparents is visitation rights after the marriage is dissolved or there is a legal separation. Once again, the rights of visitation for a stepparent are likely to be available only in a state in which the legislature has provided these rights and then only if a court determines that such is in the best interests of the child. The stepparent has to apply through the courts to establish these visitation rights.

There are also a few cases in which stepparents have obtained custody instead of a natural parent. For example, decisions in Idaho in *Stockwell v. Stockwell* (1989) and in Illinois in *In re Carey* (1989) awarded custody of a child to a stepparent instead of a natural parent. However, in Florida in *Webb v. Webb* (1989), a lower court award to a stepparent was reversed by the court of appeals (Freed & Walker, 1991).

The question of the rights and responsibilities of stepfamilies is gaining increasing national attention. The Family Law Section of the American Bar Association prepared a resolution, published in the spring of 1991, that presented a model act establishing the rights and duties of stepparents (Tenenbaum, 1991). Issues identified by the Family Law Section included concern that establishing particular rights and responsibilities could deter some couples from marriage because the couple would not want to encounter additional responsibilities and concern that the Act could cause further confusion when the natural parent has joint custody. Among other issues were the stepparent's right to discipline the children, the stepparent's obligation to support a child, and visitation rights of stepparents in the event of dissolution of marriage, legal separation, or annulment between the custodial parent and the stepparent. As the number of stepfamilies continues to increase, familiarity with these issues becomes necessary for professional counselors.

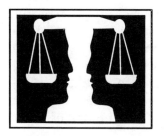

Insurance Fraud

One of the ways a marriage and family counselor may personally interact with the law regarding treatment of clients is through the legal requirement that health care providers must act in accordance with health insurance provisions of the law. An abuse of health insurance by intentionally reporting to an insurance company that a situation occurred that did not occur, for purposes of financial benefit, may be fraud. Fraud and abuse of health insurance are prohibited by law. The sanctions that might be taken against a professional counselor practicing marriage and family counseling for fraudulent reporting to an insurance company could have an adverse impact on his or her license. Additionally, the insurance company may be able to file a civil action for recovery of funds misspent and request criminal action be brought by the state, the local district attorney's office, or the county attorney.

Needless to say, the best thing to do is to not engage in fraudulent activity. In fraudulent activity five elements must be present:

1. There is false representation or concealment of a material fact.
2. This representation or concealment is reasonably calculated to deceive.
3. It is made with intent to deceive.
4. It does in fact deceive.
5. It results in damage to the injured party. ("Case Notes," 1985–1986)

Professional counselors may be tempted to misreport to an insurance company in cases in which the insurance company covers therapy for an individual but not for the family. There is an obvious frustration associated with such a limitation. Therapists may strongly believe it is a significant error by the insurance company to limit reimbursement to only individual therapy. Nevertheless, the therapist is powerless to change that particular situation and must simply abide by the rules of the insurance company. Signing insurance forms that, for example, state that you saw only John when you saw both John and Mary, or knowingly making any other form of false statement with the intention of receiving payments from the insurance company that otherwise would not be sent, may be determined to be fraud and prohibited by law.

Other areas of insurance fraud that are practiced but forbidden include (1) indicating that a psychiatrist or psychologist is rendering mental health services when a different person actually is providing the counseling, (2) rebelling against the requirement of a diagnosis by giving most or all clients the same diagnosis, and (3) purposefully forgiving or waiving the client's share of the fee while reporting the full sum to the insurance company.

The sanctions that a therapist may undergo for such actions are severe. If you ever feel tempted to "bend the rules," consider the potential long-term legal and ethical consequences before you do so.

 # Paradoxical Interventions

Some courts have found that certified marital and family therapists fall within the statutory definition of health care providers and thus are a part of the group subject to malpractice actions ("Case Notes," 1985–1986). A malpractice action is one designed to show damages for personal injury or death arising out of the furnishing of or the failure to furnish professional services by a health care provider. Even if an action labeled *malpractice* cannot be brought in some states, other actions such as negligence or infliction of emotional distress could be possible (Hopkins & Anderson, 1990).

A predominant theory used in medical malpractice actions is *negligence*. Other theories supporting legal malpractice claims may include the following:

- breach of duty to maintain the patient's trust and confidence
- use of a procedure not within the realm of accepted professional practice
- use of a technique in which the therapist was not trained (professional competence)
- failure to follow a procedure that would have been more helpful
- failure to obtain informed consent
- failure to explain the possible consequences of treatment. (Hopkins & Anderson, 1990)

The standard of care that the health care provider should provide is established by testimony presented by other practitioners in that particular field of practice or by other witnesses who are familiar and competent to testify regarding the particular field or practice. Four elements must be present in order to show malpractice (Schultz, 1982):

1. An established counselor-client relationship is present.
2. Conduct by the counselor is deemed below an acceptable standard of care.
3. Injury to the client was caused.
4. Actual injury occurred.

One area that may be particularly sensitive to malpractice is implementation of the paradoxical procedures used by some professional counselors practicing marriage and family counseling. Paradoxical procedures were first identified by Haley (1976), who suggested two major types of directives: "(a) telling people what to do when the therapist wants them to do it, and (b) telling them what to do when the therapist does *not* want them to do it, because the therapist wants them to change by rebelling" (p. 52).

A paradoxical intervention might take place when, for example, a counselor working with a constantly fighting couple tries many direct interventions, meets with no cooperation, and then finally says, "I think this fighting is very important to both of you, and I want you to continue to fight at least as much as you have in the past, if not more, until our next session." Paradox is further explained in Fraser (1984), and ethical concerns together with suggested actions are discussed by Solovey and Duncan (1992).

One ethical concern is whether the counselor is deceiving or harming clients. Selective disclosure, when used in order to employ the paradoxical intervention, is an ethical and legal concern. Another ethical concern is that the counselor may not be able to determine how a relationship system will respond to a given intervention. Furthermore, such a procedure could increase the couple or family's dependence on counseling. Nevertheless, many argue that the use of paradox is an important procedure in marriage and family counseling/therapy.

Legally, the question of the use of paradoxical therapy is important to a professional counselor seeing a couple or family if the client asserts either a violation of contract or malpractice. A violation of the contract may be created by violation of the disclosure agreement. Thus if a marriage and family counselor intends to use paradoxical therapy, the counselor should include in his or her disclosure statement paradoxical therapy among therapeutic interventions that might be used—particularly if state law requires identifying the types of therapy used—even though the counselor may believe that revealing the use of paradox interferes with the value of the intervention. Many states have laws requiring that clients have a right to choose the type of counseling and therapy they want, so the counselor may need to discuss as well as disclose therapy types. In general, counselors are protected when clients read, discuss, and sign the counselor's disclosure statement because the clients are likely to have also waived their rights to claim later that paradoxical therapy was a violation of contract.

The other type of liability that a marriage and family counselor/therapist might create by use of paradoxical therapy is tort liability or the "civil wrong that does not arise out of contractual liability" (Huber & Baruth, 1987, p. 118). The unintentional torts claimed against a therapist could be presented in a malpractice action. The four points for establishing malpractice have already been noted. The standard of care that the counselor owes the clients is established through testimony in any malpractice action, and may be limited to other practitioners in the same "school" and same geographical area. It may be difficult for the counselor/therapist to convince a judge or jury that it is acceptable practice to tell a client to do something the counselor did not want them to do, especially if the client is harmed as a result.

Furthermore, courts are taking an increasingly national view of these professions. Many state courts now consider published professional organization standards. Such standards as the *Ethical Standards* (AACD, 1988), the *Ethical Principles of Psychologists* (American Psychological Association, 1981), or the *Code of Ethics* (American Association for Marriage and Family Therapy, 1991) can be used as a criteria for judgment.

Given that there are identified ethical concerns regarding use of paradoxical therapy, a professional counselor should be careful in employing such practice. Part of that caution should, as already noted, particularly include full disclosure to the client through the disclosure statement and sufficient discussion about the type of counseling/therapy offered to insure the client's understanding and agreement to the procedure.

As Corey, Corey, and Callanan (1988) discussed in their case book on ethical standards, manipulation can be seen as an unethical behavior. The purpose of all types of psychotherapy is to help people to become able to help themselves. To avoid any suggestion of manipulation, being honest with the client is essential.

One of the best ways counselors/therapists can protect themselves from a malpractice action is to take the preventative measures mentioned here and be certain they are acting within the scope of their competence. Another way is to use personal and professional honesty and openness with clients. These concerns of honesty and openness must be carefully incorporated with any use of paradoxical therapy. If doubtful of the use of a particular intervention, seek peer consultation or supervision and perhaps legal advice before proceeding.

# Frequently Asked Questions

Q. I have been seeing this couple for several months, and they have decided on a divorce. The wife wants me to testify for her in the hearing, but the husband doesn't. What should I do?

A. If you do not have prior written permission from both parties, you should refuse to testify and explain your reasons. Check your state law to ascertain your legal position. If you are subpoenaed to testify and bring your documents, show up at the specified time with *all* documentation and ask for the judge to rule on the issue. If the court orders you to testify, then you are legally required to do so. Legal consultation is advised for all situations involving subpoenas.

To avoid both legal and ethical dilemmas, it is important to explain that as a marriage and family counselor the couple or the family is considered to be your client, rather than any individual within the unit. To reduce any later confusion, this should be in writing in your disclosure form and given to your client(s) before counseling begins.

Q. I am interested in assisting the divorcing couples that I counsel in the best possible manner. I know my state law, and I think I could save them unnecessary expense by working with them on settlement, custody, and visitation issues. Is this legal?

A. Your client's best interest is always of importance to you as an ethical counselor. You may best assist your clients through mediation with their negotiation of these matters, thus allowing less time to be spent with the legal process. Remember always that giving legal advice is illegal.

Q. In my practice, I see many couples who are divorcing. When the attorney calls, what should I say?

A. If you do not have prior written permission to talk with the attorney, simply state that if this person were your client, without written permission you would not be able to talk with the attorney. If the attorney persists, be polite but give no further information or indication of your relationship with the person in question.

Q. Why do attorneys "attack" therapists when they cross-examine them on the stand?

A. Whether you are called to testify in a case or choose to be a witness or child custody evaluator, it is important to understand the nature of the legal system. The legal system is an adversarial one, set up to discover the facts in a given situation. It is not based upon the assumption of furthering anyone's mental health or growth. The opposing attorney is merely "doing his or her job" in search of the facts, and none of the questions should be taken as being personal.

Q. What is the difference between a subpoena and a court order?

A. A subpoena is an order by an attorney for information or testimony. The order to appear in a subpoena must be followed. A court order is a directive by the court to comply and must be followed.

Q. Several of my colleagues have become "expert witnesses." Are there educational or training requirements for being an expert witness? How can I become one?

A. Your educational background and clinical expertise in a given area may qualify you to be an expert witness. Some states specify requirements for particular types of issues that must be met to qualify to testify. You may contact colleagues who are presently giving expert witness testimony or local attorneys in your area.

Above all, if you decide to become an "expert," be sure that you have sufficient knowledge in that area.

Q. I have been requested to complete a child custody evaluation for a district court. The parents are paying for the evaluation. Whom do I represent?

A. A court-appointed child custody evaluator is responsible for representing the child and the court. The evaluator is asked to determine the best interests of the children.

Q. In my marriage and family training program I learned the technique of using paradox. However, I still feel somewhat uncomfortable with this method. Are there any legal restrictions on using paradoxical interventions?

A. There are no legal restraints differing from those applying to other forms of practice. The authors caution you, however, to indicate in your disclosure statement that paradoxical interventions are part of your therapeutic technique and to be certain you are adequately trained and have sufficient facts.

It may be difficult to explain harm caused to clients by asking them to do the activity that you did not want them to do. Extreme caution is advised in the use of paradoxical interventions.

Q. What do I tell my clients who are stepparents concerning their legal rights and responsibilities toward their stepchildren?

A. Stepparents in today's society have few legal rights or responsibilities toward their stepchildren. However, some states now have a provision that recognizes the "psychological/extended family of children" and may address stepparent issues. Families should check with an attorney to understand fully their rights and responsibilities.

Q. Am I required to be licensed as a marriage and family therapist in order to see couples and families?

A. Some states require a professional to hold a license before providing mental health services, particularly in a private practice setting. In other states, licenses or certifications are optional and regulate the use of mental health titles only. You are cautioned to follow the laws of the state in which you practice.

If you are working under the auspices of an agency, school, or hospital, you may not be required to be licensed. The best advice is to check your state law.   *

Q. When I am seeing a couple or a family, is it illegal to receive insurance reimbursement for an individual client within the family?

A. It may be considered insurance fraud to submit an individual diagnosis for third-party payment when you are actually seeing a couple or family. Report honestly to the insurance company even if the result is denial of reimbursement. Fraud could result in ethical censure and/or civil and criminal liability.

 # Guidelines
for Practice

When you are functioning as a mediator for a divorcing couple . . .

1. Do not give legal advice. This is both unethical and illegal.
2. Refer your clients to separate attorneys for legal advice.
3. Be familiar with your state's laws in order to facilitate the negotiation process.
4. Remain impartial. This is imperative. Establish ground rules.
5. Define the issues to be settled. Facilitate management of emotions and good communication.
6. Negotiate an acceptable settlement.
7. Be appropriately available to your clients throughout the process.

When the divorce attorney calls . . .

1. If you have no written permission to release information, be professional but firm in your denial. Know your state laws regarding release of information.
2. If you have both clients' written permission to talk with the attorney, be professional, courteous, and informative.
3. If subpoenaed to appear with information, appear but wait for a court order to release information unless you have written permission from your clients to release information. NEVER alter or destroy documents that have been subpoenaed.

As an expert witness. . .

1. Understand the legal system in which you will be involved.
2. Be professional and thorough in your testimony. Be timely in court appearances and report writing.
3. Be prepared to support your conclusions with evidence.
4. Always be truthful.
5. Have a written contract defining your responsibilities and fees.
6. Discuss with the attorney what the expectations are in court; rehearse cross-examination.
7. Do not be offended or distressed by cross-examinations.

When called upon to complete a child custody evaluation. . .

1. Remember that you are a representative for the child and the court.
2. Be familiar with your state laws.
3. Be timely and professional in your evaluation, court appearance, and reporting.
4. If circumstances permit, discuss your conclusions with the parents before submitting your report to the court, but do not be swayed in your decision.

When using paradox or other techniques in counseling. . .

1. Be sure that you are well trained in the use of these techniques.
2. Disclose fully to your clients the types of therapy you provide and the possible consequences of that therapy.
3. If doubtful about using a technique, seek peer consultation or supervision.
4. Be aware that you will be held accountable for harm to a client as a result of using this technique.

If you qualify for third-party reimbursement. . .

1. Never misrepresent or conceal facts from the third-party provider.
2. Be confident of your diagnostic skills. Seek consultation or supervision if necessary.

3. Explain to your clients the reason for diagnosis and be honest about the possibility of nonreimbursement for family therapy.

 # Summary

By virtue of working with families, and given the frequent interaction families have with the law, marriage and family counselors are challenged by the need and the opportunity both to understand their own profession as mental health professionals and to have an understanding of their state's family law system. This opportunity enhances the career of the licensed professional counselor who practices marriage and family counseling. Obviously, it also poses challenges. We recommend that you consult with peers and attorneys for whom you have respect to gain an understanding of your state's family law. Furthermore, read the newspapers and other professional bulletins and journals to stay up to date on family law matters and counseling techniques as they evolve.

Determining how families are treated is an important public policy issue throughout the United States. You also may want to consider being involved in your local community or with your state legislature in addressing these important issues. It is critical that the perspective of therapists be a part of public policy decision making.

This monograph has reviewed several of the ways in which marriage and family therapists may interact with the law. Once again, we encourage you to consult with peers from different disciplines to understand and assist your clients in this multi-discipline area in the best ways possible.

 # Discussion Questions

1. There are several kinds of divorce possible, from uncontested to contested. What are the advantages and disadvantages incorporated into each level?

2. Mediation is becoming more popular today. This may be due both to the increased number of divorces and the increased costs (financial and emotional) associated with a contested divorce. What are some of the areas that are appropriate for mediation? What skills does the mediator need to possess? What is the goal of mediation? What is the relationship between the mediator/therapist and the attorney?

3. When working with couples and families, the professional counselor is likely to become involved in the legal system at some point in his or her career. Two of the more frequent involvements are in divorce and custody cases. What can the therapist do to avoid misunderstandings about release of information or testimony in these cases?

4. If a counselor refuses to testify or produce records voluntarily, and is still asked to give information or testify, what is the best method to follow if the attorney calls? If the counselor is subpoenaed? If the court orders the counselor to appear?

5. Marriage and family counseling has much expertise that is of value in domestic relations cases today. Becoming an expert witness can be a rewarding change for the therapist from day-to-day clinical practice. What is the difference in an expert witness and a lay witness? What is the process through which a professional counselor becomes an expert witness?

6. Child custody evaluations are also very important in today's society. As a representative of the children and the court, what are your responsibilities?

7. Paradoxical interventions are an accepted technique in strategic family therapy. What are two types of legal liabilities associated with the use of paradox? What can therapists do to protect themselves from legal charges related to use of paradox?

8. Do stepparents have legal rights? Legal responsibilities? What if a stepparent wants custody of a child after divorce? What about support responsibilities for the stepchild during marriage?

9. What are the laws regulating licensing of marriage and family therapists? Can you see families and couples without a license? What type of training is necessary for professional competence? If you are licensed in a related mental health area, can you ethically see couples and families?

10. As a licensed professional counselor practicing marriage and family counseling who qualifies for third-party payment, can you diagnose (using the DSMIII-R) one of the family members and report to the insurance company you are providing individual counseling while seeing the entire family? If you do this, will you be guilty of fraudulent reporting? What are the legal consequences of fraud?

Suggested Readings

Bautz, B. (1988). Divorce mediation: For better or for worse. *Mediation Quarterly, 22*, 51–60. This article discusses types of divorce processes and the family "types" associated with each.

Besharov, D. J. (1990). *Recognizing child abuse*. New York: Free Press. This book reviews mandatory reporting statutes and their implications for child care professionals. It has a chapter describing the primary forms of abuse and neglect, provides guidance on gaining and preserving evidence, and includes helpful tips to follow if your child is abused or if you are reported.

Fisher, M., & McFadden, L. L. (1985–1986). Premarital and remarital mediation: Complementary roles for lawyers and therapists. *Journal of Family Law, 24*, 451–479. This article gives practical information on how the attorney and the therapist can work together for the best interest of the clients.

Folberg, J. (Ed.). (1991). *Joint custody and shared parenting*. New York: Guilford Press. This book examines many of the legal as well as practical issues involved in joint custody.

Lamond, D. A. P. (1989). The impact of mandatory reporting legislation on reporting behavior. *Child Abuse and Neglect, 13*, 471–480. As laws requiring reporting are strengthened, more reports of neglect and abuse are made. This article looks at the quality of assessment in reporting.

References

American Association for Counseling and Development. (1988). *Ethical standards*. Alexandria, VA: Author.

American Association for Marriage and Family Therapy. (1991). *Code of ethics*. Washington, DC: Author.

American Psychiatric Association. (1987). *Diagnostic and statistical manual of mental disorders* (rev. 3rd ed.). Washington, DC: Author.

American Psychological Association. (1990). *Ethical principles of psychologists* (amended June 2, 1989). *American Psychologist, 45*, 390–395.

Arthur, G. L., & Swanson, C. D. (1993). *Confidentiality and privileged communication* (ACA Legal Series, Vol. 6). Alexandria, VA: American Counseling Association.

Berger, M., & Dammon, C. (1982). Live supervision as context, treatment, and training. *Family Process, 21*, 337–344.

Besharov, D. J. (1990). *Recognizing child abuse*. New York: Free Press.

Case notes (1985–1986). *Journal of Family Law, 24*, 552–558.

Child Abuse Prevention and Treatment Act of 1974, 42 U.S.C. § 5102(1) (1974).

Colorado Revised Statutes, 19-4-102.

Corey, G., Corey, M. A., & Callanan, P. (1988). *Issues and ethics in the helping professions*. Pacific Grove, CA: Brooks/Cole.

Davis, L. (1991). *Allies in healing*. New York: Harper Perennial.

Derdeyn, A. (1989). The postdivorce family. *Children Today, 18*, 12–14.

Everett, C. A., & Volgy, S. S. (1983). Family assessment in child custody disputes. *Journal of Marital and Family Therapy, 9*(4), 343–353.

Fisher, M. S., & Fisher, E. O. (1982). Toward understanding working relationships between lawyers and therapists in guiding divorcing spouses. *Journal of Divorce, 6*, 1–15.

Fraser, J. S. (1984). Paradox and orthodox: Folie à deux? *Journal of Marital and Family Therapy, 10*(4), 361–372.

Freed, D. J., & Walker, T. B. (1991). An overview. *Family Law Quarterly, 24*(4), 309–314.

Gold, L. (1981). Mediation in the dissolution of marriage. *The Arbitration Journal, 36*(3), 9–13.

Group for the Advancement of Psychiatry (1991). *The mental health professional and the legal system*. New York: Brunner/Mazel.

Haley, J. (1976). *Problem-solving therapy*. New York: Harper & Row.

Herrmann, M. S., McKenry, P. C., & Weber, R. E. (1979). Mediation and arbitration applied to family conflict resolution: The divorce settlement. *The Arbitration Journal, 34*, 17–21.

Hopkins, B. R., & Anderson, B. S. (1990). *The counselor and the law* (3rd ed.). Alexandria, VA: American Association for Counseling and Development.

Hopkins, P. E. (1982). Evaluative mediation: Upholding the child's best interests. *Conciliation Courts Review, 20*(2), 63–70.

Huber, C. H., & Baruth, L. G. (1987). *Ethical, legal, and professional issues in the practice of marriage and family therapy*. Columbus: Merrill.

In re Carey, 188 Ill.App.3d 1049, 544 N.E.2d 1293 (1989).

Knaub, K. K. (1986). Domestic relations—child support—equitable estoppel may be applied to prevent stepparent from denying obligation to support stepchildren after divorcing natural parent (Case note). *Seton Hall Law Review, 16*, 127–149.

Margolin, G. (1982). Ethical and legal considerations in marital and family therapy. *American Psychologist, 37*(7), 788–801.

Meyerstein, I., & Todd, J. C. (1980). On the witness stand: The family therapist and expert testimony. *The American Journal of Family Therapy, 8*(4), 43–51.

Miller v. Miller, 97 N.J. 154, 478 A.2d 351 (1984).

Pasley, K. (1988). Contributing to a field of investigation. *Journal of Family Psychology, 1*(4), 452–456.

Pearson, J., & Thoennes, N. (1982). The benefits outweigh the costs. *Family Advocate, 4*(3), 26–35.

Pollack, G., & Levy, S. (1989). Countertransference and failure to report child abuse and neglect. *Child Abuse and Neglect, 13*, 515–522.

Prince v. Massachusetts, 321 U.S. 158 (1944).

Remley, T. P., Jr. (1991). *Preparing for court appearances* (AACD Legal Series, Vol. 1). Alexandria, VA: American Association for Counseling and Development.

Remley, T. P., Jr., & Miranti, J. (1992). Child custody evaluator: A new role for mental health counselors. *Journal of Mental Health Counseling, 13*(3), 334–342.

Schultz, B. (1982). *Legal liability in psychotherapy*. San Francisco: Jossey–Bass.

Slaikeu, K. A., Culler, R., Pearson, J., & Thoennes, N. (1985). Process and outcome in divorce mediation. *Mediation Quarterly, 10*, 55–74.

Solovey, A.D., & Duncan, B.L. (1992). Ethics and strategic therapy: A proposed ethical direction. *Journal of Marital and Family Therapy, 18*(1), 53–61.

Spencer, J. M., & Zammit, J. P. (1976). Mediation-arbitration: A proposal for private resolution of disputes between divorced or separated parents. *Duke Law Journal, 1976*(91), 911–939.

Stockwell v. Stockwell, 116 Idaho 297, 775 P.2d 611 (1989).

Tenenbaum, J. D. (1991). Legislation for stepfamilies—the Family Law Section Standing Committee report [Special issue on third-party custody, visitation, and child Support]. *Family Law Quarterly, 25*(1), 137–141.

U.S. Advisory Board on Child Abuse and Neglect (1990). *Child abuse and neglect: Critical first steps in response to a national emergency* (No. 017-092-00104-5). Washington, DC: U.S. Government Printing Office.

Victor, R. S., Robbins, M. A., & Bassett, S. (1991). Statutory review of third-party rights regarding custody, visitation, and support. *Family Law Quarterly, 25*(1), 19–55.

Weaver, J. (1986). Therapeutic implications of divorce mediation. *Mediation Quarterly, 12*, 75–90.

Webb v. Webb, 546 So.2d 1062 (Fla. Dist. Ct. App. 1989).

Woolley, J. C. (1986). Courtroom mediation: A viable alternative to the child custody trial. *Conciliation Courts Review, 24*(2), 1–6.

NOTES